# DYBBUK AMERICANA

WESLEYAN POETRY

# DYBBUK AMERICANA

JOSHUA GOTTLIEB-MILLER

Wesleyan University Press    Middletown, Connecticut

Wesleyan University Press
Middletown CT 06459
www.wesleyan.edu/wespress

Manufactured in the United States of America
Designed and composed in Adobe Text Pro and Knockout
by Julie Allred, BW&A Books, Inc.

Library of Congress Cataloging-in-Publication Data

*Names:* Gottlieb-Miller, Joshua, author.

*Title:* Dybbuk Americana / Joshua Gottlieb-Miller.

*Description:* Middletown, Connecticut : Wesleyan University Press, 2024. |

*Series:* Wesleyan poetry | Includes bibliographical references. |

*Summary:* "Poetry that wrestles with conflicting ideologies in relation to preservation of Jewish identity and tradition in contemporary American culture, using interviews, oral histories, and archival materials"
— Provided by publisher.

*Identifiers:* LCCN 2024005617 (print) | LCCN 2024005618 (ebook) |
ISBN 9780819501158 (cloth) | ISBN 9780819501165 (trade paperback) |
ISBN 9780819501172 (ebook)

*Subjects:* LCGFT: Poetry.

*Classification:* LCC PS3607.O876 D93 2024  (print) | LCC PS3607.O876 (ebook) |
DDC 811/.6—dc23/eng/20240209

LC record available at https://lccn.loc.gov/2024005617

LC ebook record available at https://lccn.loc.gov/2024005618

5  4  3  2  1

*for* Lauren *and* Owen

# CONTENTS

**/// (Don't call me dybbuk, dybbuk says,) ///**

**/// (On the one hand, his foresight. On the other, our hindsight.) ///**

## SPIRIT, BREATH, OR WIND

I don't like to guess what kind of Jew
I could have been
in 1492, 1942; pick a year
and I would have thought, "Bad Jew,"
looking in a mirror, under my breath.
What's the prayer for that?
Sure, once the temples stood,
already ancient, scribes worked commissions,
you could have found me scrolling
through the city like an enormous smart-phone.
*If one is studying,* the sage said, *and notices
a handsome tree, a handsome field . . .
it is as if one is mortally guilty.*

The promise of divine favor I like best—
that we will be like the stars of heaven,
without count—didn't just mean looking up
in the desert at a blindfold sky,
not just multiplying like the riches
of kings or generations,
it means I belong
as much to the past
as to the future.

Telescopes use mirrors
and math to gather light
from the night sky,
and curved glass formed
from desert sands thousands
of years old, to spy stars
that still defy our count.

*But to fully understand how race or genre work, we must understand them as constructed, not natural or necessary . . .*

Brigitte Fielder

*In the process, they constructed a male-centered version of Jewishness that was prefiguratively white, and a specifically Jewish form of whiteness.*

Karen Brodkin

# DYBBUK AMERICANA

# CHAIN MIGRATION

It took ten men
to make a minyan,

but only one name
of G-d for us to share,

so we settled on
America, one by one,

we settled on America,
man and woman.

My grandfather
earned his way over

shoveling coal
in the hold of a boat.

Grandmother sewed
gold into her coat. In secret

they sewed, they sold,
they glowed. I dream of

gold. G-d's name in gold
milked and honeyed

in the dust
beneath our boots—

our dust. And when they made
a minyan and didn't

realize it? And when
they married in

and didn't realize it?
No matter: they sewed,

they sold, they glowed.
Yes, they sold

their solid gold, sold gold
into gold, sewed gold

together into dust.
When I was born

they gave me
a dead man's name.

But that's true
for everyone.

**GREAT MYSTICS,**

don't expect me to be pure.
It's Tu B'Shevat, the New Year for trees,

which is going to turn me into a liar.
This morning my son and I debated

how to look at a tree. We sat
in our gray courtyard patio

in an apartment complex in Houston's
inner loop, in, as my rabbi calls Texas,

the Promised Land. I tried
my boy's view, crouched

next to him, shouting up at the tree.
When Owen stopped laughing at me

I stopped shouting. Sometimes he asks me
whether the mind is pink or the brain

gray, or why his heart is under his neck,
pumping much fresher blood

through his body than mine ever will again.
He's surprised when I tell him what he already

knows. The sages say of one among them—
elsewise unquoted in the commentaries—

that every time his teacher began a lesson
"*G-d said,*" this curious and simple student

ran screaming in amazement.
I thumbed open my book,

but Owen's screen had faded to sleep
"because it needs to recharge,

 

I thought I'd forgotten
to read Hebrew,

I know the sounds of letters in prayers
we drag Owen to. He's confused

what the prayers are
for. He escapes

our walk back to the car
by climbing the lone fruit tree,

whose rotting unpicked oranges molder
on high branches that poke towards

the four-story parking garage.
Lauren dodges a shaking branch,

whispers to me, "I don't need
to be surrounded by trees

to be reminded that I'm judged
but the trees suffer."

We were never going to drive
into this Texas night,

and wake him up to look at the stars,
and only stop when we reached

the perfect unassuming place for
our designated mystical experience.

Lauren says, "school night." I say,
"definitely not now," and Owen

looks down on us
in the dark. I used to tell him

whatever I thought.

3

just like you. Hint hint," I said.
"But I don't have batteries in my back,"

he said. Once I knew what I thought
he could believe.

Sometimes I don't

think trees are beautiful.
He says, "I am never coming down."

## BELIEF TO ME A KIND OF SABBATH WORK

Three thousand years have I been Jewish?

> There's a Jew inside
> belief. He and I
> are prisoners—we
> share a single wall
> between our cells.
> He prays in the holy tongue.
> I don't understand.

Blinds across the windows,
cover the mirrors
when someone dies. Moses and his
technicolor sunburn coming down
from Mount Sinai.

Four thousand years? Five? When a funnel cloud touches
the ground it becomes a tornado, groping blindly down
whichever way the windstorm runs. Zeyde Phil called my sister
a tornado. "I am not a tornado,"
she wailed, five years old. How long
did I sit shiva as a baby for my grandpa?
My mother's grandma Fanny fled a village in Odessa

wiped from human maps. Her name
changed as quick

as flames forget the past. No storm chasers
in the Torah.

> (Mirchin,
> once was Merchant)

The fire

danger high above the cloud line:

> Some nights the Jew
> breaks into my cell
> and dances on my head.

the bush that when it speaks,
destroys. My ancestors were peasants
in an old cold land. Mirchins and Lezegurskis
(their children: Lezegurs, then Lessingers)

My Sabbath mind a funnel cloud
not touching the ground.

I treat my son like a golden cow.

I wonder how he's
lighter than a blessing.

## IT PRIVILEGES LAND TO SAY GHOST TREES

My son feeds egrets
pretzel sticks while I
try to remember the prayer
for throwing our sins
away with the old year.
He wants to do
everything himself.
A place is irreplaceable.
An island is a barrier
as long as it is land.

The opposite of place
is not time:

—Along tall flooded grasses
the Gulf
lines the horizon
of this pocket habitat.
Birds migrate.
Driving here
makes us tourists.—

reverse teleology:
a more accurate model
for the biological
livability of the earth.

I try to explain to my son
he needs to save me some
of our blessing. I need
forgiveness, and I am
not sure, who am I
trying to fool
with this distinction?

Barrier rigs
attract invasive corals,
lionfish, good for sport
fishing, but less biodiversity.
Even those flailing

consolations ruined
by sand-harvesting near oil rigs.
We must lament
the vanishing of the dregs
of what remains?

Our shame as partial
as our devotion.
Humans are not
the only invasive
species: we attract
and transport
islands.

Abundance, efficiency, diversity:
offsets. Look at the water
and if you don't see the birds
they aren't there.

I don't. I teach my son
about a landscape.
After the hurricane
drained back into the Gulf
the beach trash ordinary crushed
Lone Stars and dead baby sharks
washed up the same, and the birds
are here, they came to be fed,
living waters washing over
our atonement.

How can I teach a prayer
I only know how to recite?

# METROPOLIS GOLEM

Four-color avatar,
Superman doesn't have
the pronounced nose
or curly hair or skinny frame
of the   {        }famed
                        default
great American Jew.
Kansas-bred, muscled
farm-boy; there is no shame
in being the last son of a dying planet.

*Top 7 Jewish Celebrities with Gentile Names*
at Jewbellish
but *Jews who change their names*
*from Jewish names to white names*
at Stormfront. RealJewNews,
by Nazis.
JewornotJew.com,
more kosher than it sounds.

Jerome Siegel
Joseph Shuster
Robert Kahn
Milton Finger

William Eisner
Jakob Kurtzberg
Stanley Lieber

Kryptonite is a reminder of home,
radioactive poison;
he knows no old songs to fill
his stone strong lungs.

Magneto more
mutant
than Jewish?

Gottlieb =
    {      } G-d
            lover?
    G-d's love?

Stage names, pen
names,
screen names, ring
names,
code names
and alter egos.

Cut off
from my own
legend.

My son's
Hebrew name
is Yosef, but he
doesn't know it yet.

## FANTASY IMAGES

"I did— I did tell you— when they were all
    sleeping in this one apartment. That everything became
    a bed. The floor was—"

(No—)

"a bed. The ironing board was a bed. The chair
was a bed because it was so many kids
in this very small apartment. And— my father
always told the story of when he was sleeping
with brothers— his brother Jack on the floor,
and there was another— man there.
So Frank thought it was Jack's friend
and Jack thought it was Frank's friend,
and in the morning they said, 'Why did you
invite another one?'
Because we didn't know who then—
they still didn't know who this was— like—"

(Oh my goodness.)

"But you know—"

(In their home?)

"In their home, yeah. You know they would bring home friends to—
a boarder would come in, you know— to pay them a dollar
to sleep
on the floor. And— I— I don't think that children today
or people recognize the—
the greatness— of immigrant society.

"They were very brave, very brave, very brave,
very gallant.

. . . "You know don't forget they all spoke Yiddish, so there
was already commonality, and you know if you speak Yiddish
you're part of the tribe,
so— this is how they— you know—"

Two Jews,
three opinions

The outsider
within

One relative,
when I told him
who I was:

"I think you're
full of shit"

## SILENT PARTNER

According to the angels
gossiping about us,
if all Jews practice the Sabbath
at the same time, the messiah will come.
Out of the corner store, out of the warehouse
and the boxing ring, out of the showroom,
working nights and weekends and
they can't touch you, the angels.
They get as close as they can.
For weak eyes
customs agents turned away
the Talmud scholar
I descended from
(Ellis Island);
but not his son, the boxer—
in England for money in the ring,
then in America with anyone
bigger than him
who told him so—
one day he'd buy a dance
with Ginger Rogers,
queens would wear his furs
on *Queen for a Day*.

He worked his way back
and forth across the Atlantic.
He'd serve as a cabin boy,
it was easier that way
to smuggle his brothers over.

Once on his way back from England
he ran into one of his customers.
She said "Mr. Gottlieb"
and he said no, that wasn't his name.
He gave a different name.
That wasn't who he was.
And he had her convinced
that somewhere he had a twin,
because that wasn't him.
And when he went back to work

and she came to his showroom
she had the most amazing story to tell him
about the person she ran into on the ship
that looked exactly like him.
You know, he couldn't have been him.
No, no it wasn't him.
I don't think he ever told her.
I don't think I ever told you that story.

Purim is taught
as a story of passing.
Esther keeps her Jewishness
secret when she marries the king,
at her cousin Mordechai's command.
Esther reveals to the king
she is a Jew only when
the king's man, Haman,
plans to massacre us.

*It enters, for example,*
*into a home*
*with a neglected mezuzah,*
*because it knows someone*
*resides here*
*who is lax*
*in spiritual practice*
*and development.*

Purim you get so drunk
you can't tell your neighbor
from a stranger,
Haman from Mordechai,
as if in your joy
and wild abandon
you can't tell if you
are blessing Haman
and cursing Mordechai.

## MEET THE TEACHERS NIGHT

Our synagogue's security service
is employed by the father of a current student,
the rabbi joked, "so they protect the kids
as if they are their own."
After pre-school the children hide
where bushes clarify a dark metal fence,
take turns looking for each other.
When it's nice out the all-day kids come
press their faces to the bars.
"I hate that it's fenced in," Jordan says,
"When I was 10 my mother came home
from teaching here to tell me about swastikas
on the walls, swings and monkey bars
and the merry-go-round burned down."

I am learning old news is passed along
like this, if at all, after a procession
of subordinate clauses, watching
so the other parents won't hear.

I find

> I search "temple emanu el houston defaced by swastikas"
> About 9 results (0.49 seconds)
> most: Missing: ~~defaced swastikas~~
>
> I search "temple emanu el houston playground burned down"
> About 2,980,000 results (0.75 seconds)
> most: Missing: ~~playground burned down~~

"threat

chronology: jewish communal security - JCRC-NY,"

bomb threats to Owen's pre-school 68 pages in.

<table>
<tr><td>NEWSDESK</td><td>ADL Audit Shows Anti-Semitic Incidents Up In 1994</td></tr>
<tr><td>Export Citation</td><td>Violence, Personal Assaults and Arson Increase</td></tr>
<tr><td>The Forward</td><td>Export Citation</td></tr>
<tr><td>March 4, 2005</td><td>U.S. Newswire</td></tr>
<tr><td>Section: News; Pg. 4</td><td>February 15, 1995</td></tr>
<tr><td>Length: 1027 words</td><td>Section: NATIONAL DESK</td></tr>
<tr><td></td><td>Length: 1560 words</td></tr>
</table>

Once I ran into the garage to stop a little girl who bolted when her mother looked the other way. I was just quick,

| The doors of Congregation Brith Shalom in Bellaire and **Houston**'s Congregation **Emanu El** were scratched with swastikas and with the words "Jews Die" and "Aliens." | Molotov cocktails were thrown at the main building of the Jewish Community Council in Corpus Christi, Texas; Congregation **Emanu El** in **Houston**, and **Temple** Beth David in Snellville, Ga. |
|---|---|

     we'd all have done it.
     I ask around
     about the arson.
     No one else knows,
     not even rumor
     and lore.

I don't want to scare anyone.

A friend who works here
tells me not to worry.
"We have more to fear
from a random shooting."

CONQUISTADORS

Two Torahs
exist in any one
Torah, equal
and simultaneous,
written and
spoken. Two
Torahs exist in
any Jew.

They'd fled the Inquisition
all the way to Texas,
which didn't yet exist . . .

1492,
(Jews expelled
from Spain)
sailed the ocean
blue.

New Christians, they'd advanced far
within the New World.
Their patriarch—Luis de Carvajal—
governor of a province;
it's possible he might have been Christian
after all, if only New.

Lineages
traced across
five centuries sing
five millennia
of kinship with
our forebears.
It was
rumored then
that some
survived.

One telling blames rivals
who lusted after his riches.
In another, he's given up
by his own nephew, a boy
caught performing the daily ritual life
of a false convert,
tortured into a confession.
The boy names his whole family.

Still other Jews were hired on
by illiterate conquistadors
as records-keepers, skilled bricklayers
and bakers, multilingual,
clerically formalizing
land deals in Latin. Not
easily identifiable Jews.

In Spanish Texas they closed the blinds,
hummed a melody each Friday night,
recited words long-severed from meaning,
or kept a kind of kosher,

more than me.

I too hum along.
Prayers, inheritances
I open up inside me,
blank.

His auto-da-fe,
whipping,
    burning at the
        stake.

In his place I like to imagine Columbus
as Converso, Marrano, Crypto-Jew.

America, whose death
didn't you come from?

## ROTHKO BEFORE THE COLOR FIELDS

Twenty-five years after his arrival, Marcus Rothkowitz
became an American citizen
and, two years later, he was Mark Rothko.
He also left behind his first wife.

Are you who you are,
or who you were supposed to be?
What does revision

*In place of the realistic genre scenes that had dominated his work, Rothko turned to 'tragic and timeless'
themes from Greek mythology and Christian iconography, which he combined with subtle references to
Jewish burial practices and the Holocaust.*

have to do with authenticity?
My poetry has always been
more Jewish than me.

And yet, I am most drawn to his invention
of suffering, to the incident which is
now always portrayed as his act
of imaginative Jewishness:

*Although there were apparently no pogroms in Dvinsk at that time, Rothko's awareness of such events
was nonetheless very real—many years later, the artist even described a scar on his nose as the result of
Cossack violence.*

It is hard to parse the layers of that scar.

## REJECTED JEWISH GIRLS

In Fort Worth Rabbi Fox warned
of *"white slaves,*
*the large number of Jewish prostitutes*
*in the city."* Rabbi Fox:
*"Ranchmen were heard to make*
*remarks in hotels and drugstores*
*about the 'Jew whores.'"*

*Customs agents rejected Jewish girls*
*as morally defective, at Galveston*
*deported more than four times*
*the number of female Jewish immigrants*
*than did their colleagues in New York*
*between 1907 and 1913.*

"One of the reasons
they came over
was they had
a lot of problems
with pogroms
and the Cossacks
and she talked once
about the girl next to her
shot while she was in school.

"They had to hide.
We could not have a gun
in our house.
We played cowboys
and cowgirls
and we weren't allowed
to have guns,
we would have anything

She was supposed to be sent for,
but my great-great-grandma Rachel
couldn't wait.

"She picked up all the kids
and took them across."

In steerage. "If it wasn't for grandma Fanny
they would have all probably perished.
Mingling up on deck
with the paying passengers,
charming them, spiriting food
back to the hold. She had a way
of just mingling,
getting to know people.
When she was on,
she was a livewire."

They landed in New York.
A year later 'The Galveston Plan'
would have led them to Texas:
Fanny could be rejected

but. She was very
anti-gun,
anti-war,
anti-military,
you name it."

as a criminal, or a radical,
called a whore,
after the years-long
journey from Russia.

Rabbi Fox warns of "*realities*
*and the exaggerated rumors they inspired.*"

# HOW TO READ THE DYBBUK

*"I wouldn't want to be a member of any club that would have me,"* I'd say to family and friends,

thinking that if they laughed I would get it. *Duck Soup* and *Animal Crackers* and *A Night at the Opera*;

alone in my basement with those old movies, Groucho Marx epitomized class.

In my proudly self-

I thought I did get it,

funny.

deprecating teenage years,

though I was less and less

I remembered

the joke

They've got me all wrong—
the movies, magic books—
dybbuk says, steal
your body, sure, when you're
weak, spiritually vulnerable,
dead,       but dybbuk's
just *a sinner seeking refuge.*

reading about

European academies,

opposite of the ghettoes.

exclusive

Of course, Groucho must have been

referring to that antiquity.

But he was talking about Hillcrest,

I'd later learn: the club for Hollywood Jews.

A demon, sure,
climbing one more rung
of the afterlife ladder.
*SEE DEATH:*
*GHOST: POSSESSION. GHOSTLY.*
Striving to attain
a higher degree of being.

Hillcrest's

glamour

grew

with its

members'

fame,

Dybbuk calls me putz,
schmuck, schlemiel—the truth
changes you and then
you must learn it again—
fercockt, dybbuk calls me,
eats my challah, drinks my wine,
angry I won't let him go.

but its prestige came first

as a refuge for old

Jews whose gentility

unquestioned: some

California clubs of

The California Club.

European

with prohibitions

as members, of, for instance,

You're obsessed, dybbuk says,
and sits down heavy
and ashamed
he's stuck with me.
To keep kosher
the container also
has to stay pure.

German and Dutch

had long been

had helped found

status, for instance,

The arrival of Eastern

coreligionists coincided

against any Jews

The California Club.

So Hillcrest, founded by German and Dutch Jews, bankers and lawyers,
meant to preempt and exclude Hollywood Jews.
Their timing was a joke:
the Depression forced old families
to admit their social lessers.

In this meandering way, layers of exclusion and race-consciousness circle each other like talismanic leaves manic in the wind, scorched blue sky electric, Harpo Marx running around a Hillcrest golf tournament in a gorilla suit, as if cracking a spell.

And, of course, Groucho was a member.

*"Ethnicity" is a relatively new word, coming into use mainly after World War II. It replaced "people" and "nation" and served as an alternative to "race," which was associated with biology, eugenics, and other theories of scientific racism. In this discourse, "ethnicity" emphasized cultural attributes in contrast to biological ones. More recently, "ethnicity" has been used to describe the cultural heritage of Europeans, while "race" has been used for everyone else.*

The phrase 'white trash' can be rejected either in terms of race or class: white trash meaning either 'white, but trash,' or 'not white, because trash,' the rare instance where addition serves as subtraction.

*That is, did money whiten? Or did being incorporated into an expanded version of whiteness open up the economic doors to middle-class status? Clearly . . .*

white
**Origin:** A word inherited from Germanic.

*adj.* Of the lightest colour possible, that of milk or freshly fallen snow; designating this colour.
    In many instances designating things which only approximate to this colour.

*v.*
    **1.** *intransitive*
    (*a*) To become or grow white; to assume a white colour or appearance. (*b*) To be white.

    **2.** *transitive*
    (*a*) To give a white colour or appearance to; to cause to grow or become white.

///

*not-quite-white not-bright-white,*
*considerably whitened by this time,*
*no longer off-white, not-yet-fully-white,*
*postwar whitening,*

*white by submersion in an expanded notion*
*of whiteness, the whitening process,*
*the old white and the newly white*
*the white welcome wagon*

*honorary whiteness,*
*socially sanctioned whiteness*
*"White man's work"*

*white entitlement*
*a whiteness of our own*
*the emptiness of whiteness*

When it's me telling the story,
I have to take a long look
in that mirror.

## MICROWAVE

I was taking the two minutes to microwave a Trader Joe's frozen burrito
in the kitchen that was also a dining room that was also a mail room
for this branch of the state community college
when the campus executive,
who had walked in with a friend he'd been chatting with about horse politics,
said, "He's a Jew but he's really a nice guy."
We were the only ones in the break room.
They raised glazed donuts to their fat lips.
I thought, 'fat lips?' and I looked around for the blonde women
whose chatter I often enjoyed,
Sues and Annes and Peggys I liked despite
having nothing in common aside from this room, but it was just me
and this bearded administrator, balding
and in my memory he could have been talking to anyone
but I didn't want to stare. I know the microwave
shined its light behind me until it beeped and I opened it.
I looked past them, out the windows that led to the playground
that butted up against our school.
Later I would drive by mothers waiting in their cars watching their children
file out with their teachers.
Whenever I remembered this moment,
looking back, it was always about looking forward,
the long commute home, the roads that opened up to horizon
where I'd round a bend and fields would flower,
the leaves different there: Red Oak, Valley Forge, Elm,
and Autumn Fantasy Maple. My mind would work its way back
to that closet of a community college Writing Center
where I'd sit all morning, all afternoon,
rural expanse far north of Madison, where I lived,
but not where I was from. When students didn't show
I graded papers or wrote poems; the commute was worth it
for all the free time. It was a good job,
I thought, as I sat with my burrito at my computer.
I didn't care. And that was the truth, too. I didn't care about them,
I didn't care enough about what they thought or had to say,
I didn't think it mattered.

## WHITE ETHNICS

Before we were white we weren't Jews,

The day after the massacre my family and I
hear scattered reports from our friend whose
parents worship at Tree of Life,
his childhood synagogue. We are driving
home from a conference, and on the way
we stop at Lady Bird Johnson Wildflower
Center. Sunday afternoon, a wedding
is about to start. Men wearing yarmulkes
and suits carry in grocery-store flowers,
a bride ushered through the mazes
of plants while the men look at their shoes.
Are they wearing kippahs in solidarity?
Is the wedding about to begin?

We are already leaving, back to Houston;
walking out I push Owen's tiny green
stroller around the black Suburban blocking
the crosswalk, and since the driver has his
window down, I mutter, "You're blocking
the crosswalk, bud."

"You don't have to be rude," he says.

"Just letting you know," I say, looking
back over my shoulder.

"Let's talk about it, let's settle this,"
he says, finally pulling out of the crosswalk.
He has to find a parking space so we pretend
we didn't hear, hadn't bothered strapping
Owen in and Lauren's hurrying him over
the rocky walkways between the aisles of
parked cars while I scan the turns in front of
us. "You don't pick fights with white guys in
black Suburbans" Lauren hisses at me, loud
enough only for me
to overhear, and Owen,
the parking lot labyrinthine.

we were Hebrews. It's Hebrews
restricted on deeds in River Oaks,
Hebrews in scattered
news clippings before the Civil War,
after Texas was America. Not Jews,
America, but Hebrews lined
in gray and blue, though most
civilians fled Houston by 1862.
Loyalty was not for Union
or Rebel ideals: we fought
for our neighbors.

Before we were white
as what you're not, absence
of black or brown
or anything else. Not
Italian, not Irish, not
from here,
we were Hebrews.

///

Tree of Life
is a reminder that ideas
are made dangerous
by those who think them.

White as scarcity,
"Jew will not replace us."
"You also had some very fine people
on both sides."
Before we were lonely

as the color white,
white as an idea, passing
as pejorative, an assault on an idea.
To be murdered as an idea.

Jewish also as an idea,

hence the ability to pass.
Hence the danger posed by
conspiracy.

Non-white as in contamination of,
as in two drops of blood,
as in my son Owen
will always be Jewish.

///

Our car is in a corner spot tucked away in
the shade. They're both buckled and I am
struggling to fit the stroller in the back with
all our luggage when I see a black SUV
cruising towards us, I'm closing the back
door, I am trying to close the back door,
pushing the stroller and the picnic basket
and our bags hard away from the
latch which doesn't want to catch.

In 1915 the news says lynched
when Leo Frank is dragged out of jail
and murdered by southern gentlemen,
but when white supremacists
bomb The Temple,
in nearby Atlanta, by 1958
they are believed to be retaliating
against the outspoken civil rights advocacy
of the synagogue's rabbi.
Their Jewishness by then almost
beside the point.

From inside the wreckage:
charred remains veil live oaks,
hanging down where the wall's been
torn off, bricks spilling like roses
into a bright-white sky.

///

Juxtapose the sheer amount of children's Holocaust literature I read as a boy with my failure to
understand anti-Semitism as anything but a history lesson.

I grew up in a suburb of our nation's capital. It felt like living in the future. Still my friends told
stories after Sunday school that were as fantastic as comic books: other little boys checking under

their curls for horns, throwing pennies at their feet, teaching them jokes about ovens and dead babies. Where did they cook this stuff up?

The Holocaust was supposed to be, after an abomination, instructive as a horrific and consuming aberration.

For me millennia of anti-Semitism were blotted out by Nazis. Anything less than genocide seemed uneventful. Pogroms, Inquisition, the Crusades; ghetto at first a legal and official distinction, then descriptive, and only finally colloquial; beneath that the word 'Semite' itself derogatory, applied first by non-Jews.

///


Sometimes I imagine assimilation
on a scale,
like the scale justice holds.
The scale tips, blind justice
peeking under her blindfold.

///


That pause at the J as I am talking
with an older Jewish woman, a mentor,
about my newfound understanding
of our shared disinterest in whiteness

and all of its attendant advantage,
neither of us naïve about the skin
covering our bodies. We are sitting
on a bench when a janitor,
an older Black woman,
takes her break next to us.

That pause in our conversation,
when the two women chat
about their grandchildren.

After | You can be a Turkish Christian or a Chinese Muslim but not a Jewish Jew. | that

In Israel, Ethiopian and Mizrahi and Sephardic Jews see Ashkenazi Jews as white, but Ethiopian and Mizrahi see Sephardic as white, too.
There is a phrase in Israel: To become an Ashkenazi.

Genetic tests developed in America perhaps without intention find markers of Ashkenazi Jewishness simply as Jewishness.

///

My favorite story of mixed-up American names I learned from Robert, a Houstonian most directly of Canadian and Israeli heritage, who met an Irish Kramer in his business travels. This Kramer's family had moved from Ireland to Brooklyn, and thinking Kramer was a strong American name happily changed their own. Robert often travels internationally, always tells people he's Mongolian.

///

From England, from Iran, from India, many come here to escape their own racist systems. They know the Statue of Liberty, its yearning for huddled masses. They know "God Bless America." They think assimilation has meant *they invented the America they wanted to be a part of.*

///

Israelis describe America as a big brother. Suspicious of Europe, finding in America a model democracy. Israel's racial imaginary resembles America's: non-Ashkenazi welcomed into the polity at the expense of Palestinians and Arab Israelis.

the three of us

continue
to sit together,
'pause' is the wrong word.
We don't know what to say.

///

> Do you consider yourself Jewish?
> Does the community consider you Jewish?
> What rituals do you perform?
> Do you remember learning the words
> to which you lift your voice in song?

Whiteness as
"He's a striver."

To think about who you are
is to feel threatened?

///

When Lauren bought the plant
that sits in front of our apartment,
Wandering Jew, I thought the name
a metaphor for our tribal
refugee history, the welcome
we once learned not to expect.

The origin story
of the name Wandering Jew,
I now know,
is about an apostate's
supposed rejection of Jesus.

I hadn't been exposed
to that kind of calcified
almost bone-dry
invective in my diverse,
suburban neighborhood
of politely boring character.

///

White imagination
White guilt
White privilege
White supremacism

///

> And whiteness now,
> that American whiteness
> infiltrated by Jews and Catholics,
> 'Alpines' and 'Celts,' Puerto Ricans,
> East Asians, Russians,
> huddled former masses, refugees
> or bounders, the lip
> of that scale lower
> and lower, blind justice
> not blind, but blinded,
> a whiteness
> as abstract
> as the inside
> of a blindfold.

Becoming white when your parents
get a Christmas tree, when becoming white
seems nothing more
than neighborly.

///

A mixed-race writer visiting Africa asks
about Philip Roth's Coleman Silk,
from *The Human Stain*,
*Is passing an act of capitulation, or resistance?*
*A rejection of identity, or of identification?*

Roth did not want to be 'only' a Jewish author.
So he did not want to be 'a Jewish author.'

*The challenge and irony put before those who pass as white*
*is that white is an unspoken norm. Successive waves of*
*immigrants have arrived in the United States and acquired*
*whiteness . . . in order to claim it, passers have to racialise it,*
*define it, give it some sort of mass and shape.*
*They have to "act white." But is it even possible*
*to pin down an ontological whiteness?*

White benevolence
White pride
White conceit
White vainglory

///

Very occasional violence
against whites
associating with non-whites,
against Jews for associating
with non-whites or
despoiling a gentile girl.

///

The train my son loves to ride,
taking him to the Rodeo or
football or downtown, up Fannin
or down San Jacinto, stopping in
the Museum District where we
lived when we first moved to
Houston, no one mentioned
it was a Jewish neighborhood
decades before; the light train
lightly passes by the ghost of 'San
Jew-cinto' High School.

My father, born in Oklahoma,
his father in Colorado,
his grandfather
could be a justice of the peace
and judge,
when it was just a detail
not to have a law degree.
Descended across a continent
of American centuries
from Northern Europeans
("I'm Sweder
than you," he tells me).

That the American experiment
is best as a myth of possibility
just enough Americans believed,
a place where love is possible
between people who took centuries
of ancestral movement
to meet. That my mother, who came
from Jews who married Jews who
married Jews could marry my father.

My father, who might have converted
if he thought the rabbi believed in G-d.

Raised outside the faith, a friend asked
his father if he ever thought
about being Jewish.
            Surprised
when his father said, "Every day."

In narrative start as late as possible / In history as early.

"No Cossacks riding
into your mother's classrooms,"
my father says, finally,
as if I could cling to the past
he was born into,
doomed to insist
on optimism
as witness.

*To be more German than the Germans,*
*like Heine; more French than the French, like Dreyfuss,*
*Sartre, and Simone Weil; more English than the English,*
*like Disraeli; more Russian than the Russians,*
*like Isaac Babel, who rode with the Cossacks.*

*/ To believe in the host culture's own ideals*
*about itself /*

*about itself /*
*/ To believe in the host culture's own ideals*

~~It's called class-based assimilation:~~
~~Even the temples discarded like first wives.~~

"Did they tell any jokes
about the fur business?"
I asked.

"These uncles and aunts I had . . .
—You know."

"There were no fun and games
like you would know in your
family."

To haunt a ghost

appears *and* disappears.

Mid-century art critic Clement Greenberg *reduced each art medium to a critique of itself.* Painting was about flat surfaces, not narrative. *In effect, a painting, like Greenberg himself, was not supposed to have very much of a history.*

What myth is as accurate as an abstract, as exact as an extract?

When my great-aunt Edith first says her grandfather's name—'Sholem,' I hear—I regret never knowing it before we named Owen.

Sholem! One day I ask Owen if he'd want to be called Owen or Sholem. "The Hulk!" he says.

A few weeks later Edith e-mails a eulogy that mentions Sholem, only his name was Shalom.

## IS IT WRONG THAT I FIND COMFORT IN FINDING MYSELF

in the worst stereotypes?
*unwashed, uncouth, unrefined, loud*
*and pushy.*

Well.
                    *(the pushful energy!)*

*Crude vulgar* etc.

*Dirty, lascivious, immoral and either*
*knaves or fools.*
*—effeminate but lecherous knaves—*
*And the men, whether hypermasculine*
*or effeminate, all lusted after white women.*

I could be shallower, flashier,
thin my lusts.
I've been so worried
about talking over myself. But—

> "I didn't realize I was going to
> an anarchist convention,"
> my father says (his first Seder).

> *(Crude, vulgar, shallow,*
> *flashy, contrary,*
> *and galling!)*

> I sweat, I stink, I can go on
> this way, in my Jewishness,
> from parable to parable,
> but the whale isn't a metaphor
> when Jonah is in it.

> *—mean-faced,*
> *shifty-eyed, and unassimilatable*
> *[sic];*
>
> *they lie and cheat;*
> *Undersized and weak-muscled*
>
> *aggressive and coarse,*
> *as a dirty and criminal people*

even my tiny acts
of scorn
merely fulfill another
stereotype.

                    —romanticizing *On*
                    *being "too Jewish," see . . .*

> alien/even

Worried I am
only ever ashamed
paradoxically, ironically,
as though by institutions of assimilation

and uplift . . .

## CONVERSION

<table>
<tr>
<td>The creation of a word from an existing word<br><br>without any change in form+</td>
<td>Reversing the two parts of a categorical<br><br>or implicational statement+</td>
<td>Going for<br><br>two+</td>
</tr>
<tr>
<td>From one code<br><br>to another+</td>
<td>Law chemistry<br><br>arbitrage+</td>
<td>A form a funnel an<br><br>action+</td>
</tr>
</table>

---

IT'S FUNNIER WHEN LAUREN TOLD IT

"A Jewish businessman warned his son
against marrying a 'shiksa,'" she
says. "The son replied,
"But she's converting to Judaism."
"It doesn't matter," the old man said.
"A shiksa will cause problems."
After the wedding, the father called the son,
who was in business with him,
and asked him why he was not at work.
"It's Shabbos," the son replied.
The father was surprised:
"But we always work on Saturday.
It's our busiest day."
"I won't work anymore on Saturday,"
the son insisted, "because my wife
wants us to go to shul on Shabbos."
"See," the father says. "I told you
marrying a shiksa would cause problems."

The rate at which one
currency will be
exchanged

                    for another+

Changing one form of
energy

                    to another+

1+1

                    = 2/3+

I was lucky she cared/
didn't care

                    I was a Jew

The pain of

                    belonging+

Taboo, too, to say
I've always loved

                    Lauren's nose

## THE SABBATH APPROACHES

Signs say *follow signs to hidden falls*
against the sound of water
eliciting a stream coming down

right in front of me. Like when I get
the {             } letter
                    spirit

of the water
wrong, practice the Sabbath
on vacation. Jenny Lake, The Grand Tetons.

That's *The Big Teats* in French, which is
most definitely not the holy tongue.
These tourists crowd with ignorant sureness.

This waterfall reminds them how nature is
supposed to be: unhidden.
I don't want to pray

for myself, but I think I'm spinning
when I pray for anyone else.
In one father, the mountain is a mountain.

In one mountain is a midrash
on a G-d still implicit between us.
Water concentrates, becomes

the hidden falls. It is impossible
to separate my obsessions:
a G-d I never knew

from a G-d I can pass on. Blessed
and creator of the etcetera,
find us and call it prayer.

Edith: ". . . she was very young, I think she was 15 or 16, and for 5 years she didn't have a child so the rabbis told my grandfather that he could divorce her. *But he liked her.* She was very cute. And— she fooled them all. After that every single year she had a child, so she had either 11 or 12 or 13, we're really not sure— And my grandfather came to find an apartment for this enormous family and . . . he finally sent for Rachel who came with all these children, but when she came through Ellis Island and my grandfather went down to meet her she wouldn't go with him because, she said 'That's not my husband. My husband had a beard. My husband had side-locks. My husband wore a hat. Who is this man? I don't know who this man is.' And it took a while for him to convince her that he was her husband."

Thinking I'd find myself
further and further back . . .

and then thinking I had,
a scholar, a poet even . . .

". . . so the women— Anita, I'm sorry, Becky and Fanny and Gussie and Eva, they— they all chipped in and they got a little dry goods store. In New York. And they put Grandpa in there . . . They sold buttons and laces, you know little items in the store. The store was in the Bronx and the front of the store was a door, and then there was a glass top . . . so that people could look into the shop. Anyway Grandpa simply stayed in that shop, pulled down the shade in the front and proceeded to read— the Talmud and the machzor and the prayers, and teach— he taught my brother how to play chess and to read Hebrew. He never worked. He didn't— he didn't work at all."

"What a bunch of lazy old
men," my mother says.

Still the ash floats

to my surface.

## CONTINUITY THEORY

I wait tables at a novelty themed Tex-Mex restaurant, The Hobbit Café. I'm a natural hobbit, and I know my shit . . . I could pass a pin-test in *The Silmarillion*. Travis (Boromir) once asked Lauren (Arwen) if Hanukkah was when Jews celebrated Jesus's birth.

A manager (Galadriel), friendly and eager, said she was cool with Jews because "it's all the same book."

> *A shared culture, hybrid product, responsible*
> *for the colonialist project rather than itself*
> *an instance of colonization or cannibalism?*

'Well-meaning' is the phrase I am looking for.

Judaeo-Christian | Judeo-Christian, *adj.* and *n.*

    *adj.* 1. Chiefly *Church History.*

My family eats dinner with friends from work (Eowyn) whose son wears a "Victory in Jesus" t-shirt while he shivers the joystick of an arcade game, Teenage Mutant Ninja Turtles, Owen on his tippy-toes, scrapping for a turn. Donatello and Raphael keep fighting the same robots, dying and spawning; Donatello can jump and kick, but Raphael can't scroll right. They mash buttons until they get bored. I try, too, after they give up, but the kids were right, it's broken.

> 'Well-meaning,' of course, I want to say harmless.
> If anything, then, I chuckled,
> an excuse not to explain to them
> the history of religion.

If you have, as I have not, *studied much Torah,*
*you shall be given much reward.*
*Faithful is your employer to pay you the reward*
*of your labor*, Rabbi Tarfon prayed,
*And know that the grant of reward*
*unto the righteous is in the age to come.*

Even now, in the twenty-first century
of our common era, I hesitate,

searching for a clarity
delicate enough
in the comparison of fantasy texts
as a controlling metaphor:
In *The Lord of the Rings*
the Fourth Age
is *the age to come.*

What I'm talking about, on the one hand,
is tone.

It would be easier to {          } judge
justify
them if they were
'those fuckers we work for!'
but they're as well-meaning
as Tarfon,
witness to the destruction
of the second Temple,
who swore he would burn
scrolls written by heretics,
even if the name of G-d
could be caught up in the flames.

Asked what side he's from
my son says, "the middle."
His mother, his father.
"You're on the outsides."

## I WONDER AT HIS HEBREW NAME BUT DO NOT ASK

It is possible my double does not think I am his double.

This Joshua an academic, a historian. Whenever I tell people about my project they ask if I have talked with Josh. They call him Josh, like me.

Indeed I have.

The other Josh is also Jewish. He is about as new to Houston as I am. We are the same height, he is also a father, I suspect I make a better point guard, and he a less effortful lecturer.

He has researched Houston's Jewish community and created an archive to preserve its memory.

I have been in this archive.

*Since they cannot afford to have two*
*synagogues, and two rabbis,*
*most of them have one synagogue,*
*in partnership,*
*with one rabbi serving*
*both theological groups.*

Joshua?)—

I
attended
one of
his
lectures.
The
other
Josh—
(why not,

*Seated on both sides, the rabbi*
*addresses each side in turn,*
*delivers his sermons.*

maintains an observant religious practice
~~about whose rigors~~
~~I refuse to speculate~~.

Writing a Torah is a mitzvah,
the last commandment.
We read the Torah again and again,
we read the same Torah,
we make it new by listening to it.

My Hebrew name is Shraga.

"Little pig," my mother said.
Never did I hear that name
(in anger).

## A GENIZA

What could I
have said

to G-d that G-d

won't
just understand?

The secret of every parallel earth?

Nothing is different. A scientist
came upon her mirror self

in a telescope,
baffled by her confused reflection.

Geniuses found G-d
in one {          } word
world.
I am

Black holes—
denser than suns—

from

far enough,

Wisdom, cowardice,
what would I need

for to aspire to
{ } self-
discovery

to be enough?

as if from within


an ancient locker:

all that has been { } thrown out

saved in me—

worn-out books, receipts

from the marketplace, spent


prayers—for fear the Name

might go un-spared.


I don't know everything about me.

What I have learned has
been lost

before what I teach

can be
{ } lost
again

## JEWISH EXORCISM

*The Jewish Jesus*—a man in a tallit—
I've got the billboard timed
on our commute; I ask Owen
if he wants his music, point away, towards the sunset
over downtown. It nags at me, each day,

I don't want to be targeted
for conversion, but what if
the smiling billboard man
is Jewish,
like Buber, like Maimonides
writing about Jesus?

I know more of Jesus than any sage
{          } we
Jews
read today.
There are ancients whose teachings live on:
say 100 blessings a day?
Add a single letter to a single word of
Torah

and you strive to be so good?

Still I puzzle Jesus's Jewishness

from rumor and lore
written decades
after his death, canonized
over gnostic gospels
centuries later, hardening
the historical figure
into a myth.

I read Owen *Superman* comic strips,
black-and-white, whenever he wants;

he turns heavy pages
in a hardbound tome.
Superman ran *faster*
*than a speeding bullet,*
*more powerful than a locomotive.*

Man of Tomorrow, Man of Steel,

Kal-El. Costume changes
and reboots, endless planet-saving
sequels of moody self-sacrifice . . .
you remember
that only eighty years ago

he could *leap tall buildings*
*in a single bound,*
but no more?
Tremendous powers and limitations,
a few issues later transformed

into effortless flight.

And then one day he's gone,
*The Jewish Jesus* man,
tallit and all.
I had never realized before
how billboards resemble
single frozen panels
of comic books.

At night, while Lauren puts Owen to sleep,
I search his website, where
he lists his actions as crusades,
murderous medieval rampages
about which I have little to say,
except that at synagogue
when I'm told to circumcise
the foreskin of my heart,

I'll cry
when this man
is all I can I think of—
the cantor bows her head
in song—
what's in the want
of deep religious feeling
within me
lifting my voice
to follow along?

## POSSESSION

*Since all creation is engaged in the quest for perfection,*

I check O's safety belt 3 times

before we ride the Texas Flyer

230 feet above the Gulf—

suspended, panoramic, time

shorted my stare ripped

thin strap of polyester

locked to his seat and I caught

Ferris Wheel, oil derricks, skyline,

ferry, waves-waves-waves,

his screams un-broken by

anything but breath;

he told me before

not to comfort him,

he wanted to scream;

again and again my eyes

hunt his safety belt

like enlightenment.


I would not say I _____.

There's
nothing
wrong
with me,
dybbuk says.
Dybbuk says
I'm not a
prophet,
says I've
suffered
enough,
homesick
for a home
that never
was.
Dybbuk says
I'm a kite,
let G-d
do the heavy
lifting.
Dybbuk
wants to
know
why I'm
always asking
why.
And what
would having
it all
mean
for a
righteous
man?

The night before, wind stole a kite

from his hands to G-d,

nylon Iron Man shot above my head

past the seawall where it sped beyond;

~~just like that I watched him in my mind;~~

when our feet touch Pleasure Pier
again he runs to his mother, yelling,
"I almost fell into the waves!"

The month is Elul, school
starting soon, soul-searching
and confession facing
the Days of Awe. I want
that, don't I?
As the sun slips down
the other side of the island,
as a carnival surges around us,
I hold my son's hand,
point up at the Texas Flyer
once again reaching its ascent,
just before it starts to swing,
from this distance,
as if in every direction.

**NEW PRAYER BOOK**

Owen's religious school
sends us a gift
for New Year's:
a prayer book
under a letter
topped with honey sticks:
*ancient teachers*
*smeared pages of the Talmud*
*with honey*
*so children would know*
*study was sweet.*

Unearthed letter
mentions Shalom Mirchin:
*For instance, he never resented*
*going to his store*
*daily with his batch of books*
*he intended reading there.*
*He kept the door locked, for fear*
*a customer would come in.*
*And when he did make*
*a transaction, it was not always*
*profitable financially.*
*One time, when mom*
*asked him why he sold a few yards*
*of material to a woman at 7 cents*
*a yard, when it cost him 10 cents,*
*he replied, "She needed it."*

I'm greediest
on the basketball court,
for assists

*At any rate, after 5 lessons,*
*papa decided I was now ready*
*to give piano lessons myself.*
*So a large sign was put up*
*in one of our front windows, "Piano lessons—*
*25 cents an hour. PRACTICING FREE!"*
*(The come-on.) And they came alright*
*(for them, not for me) ragged, barefooted often,*
*young and old; and I tried to teach them*
*more than I knew myself. I practiced*
*and gave lessons in our bare living room.*
*But very soon, this was rented out*
*to a boarder: a violinist who gave violin lessons.*
*So my piano was moved into our adjoining*
*dining room. And when my adult pupils came*
*in evenings, for their free practicing, there were*
*invariably the visitors and the snackers*
*at the dining room table, shouting,*
*as was the custom.*

I had torn
the yellow envelope open
until my hand was sticky:
one of the honeys
had been crushed.
I suspect the tube burst
in transit, or under piles
of undelivered mail,
but I prefer to imagine
our rabbi broke it
with his thumb,
before licking
the envelope closed.

Don't call me dybbuk, dybbuk says,
          that's so "on-the-nose."
Don't put me in a box, dybbuk says,

          I'll possess the body
              of each poem.

Who's the dybbuk you or I?
Who the object, who the eye?
Who says yes and who says no?

Dybbuk wants to know.

## HOW HEROES TALK

The museum provides magnifying glasses
for the detail in the courtiers' smiles

in the illuminated manuscript. The man
next to me reads Farsi, whispers

the prince won't be allowed to become king
unless he kills the story's hero,

so the hero explains to the prince:
try it, you'll stop

the queen's heartbeat with sorrow.
Gold-flecked pages held fast in glass cages.

Tiny figures suspended between painted borders;
the greatness of the deeds they witness

prevailing across centuries.
When I leave the museum,

clouds float like students:
obscure, airy fluff over the church

across from the museum.
At night it's so dark

///

the parking lot doubles
for the moon.

When Gabe, day-shift waiter, drinking
since night-crew came on, tells me I

"should walk away," adds,
"lousy New York Jew," I tell him: "I'm glad

you've been having such a nice evening."
I'm not even from New Jersey.

His buddy Eric, fifth-generation Texas Jew,
slaps him in the face.

Wouldn't you? Six hours
they'd been wingman-ing each other,

months spotting each other
in the weight room.

"Jew pussies," Gabe says,
then just "Jews," so Eric tells Gabe

he fucked Gabe's sister "in the ass
so hard cum shot out of her nose,"

shares his opinion of her
"olive-skinned boyfriend, a terrorist

at best." After they shove each other,
Eric leers at me: "I stand

for what I believe in." Then shouts
at Gabe, "you fucking anti-Semite."

Undressing to the waist,
they circle each other three times;

Eric grabs Gabe in a headlock,
Gabe hugs Eric's torso—they shift

among shattered pint glasses,
overturned bar stools, crash-land

beneath the Christmas tree
decorating the outdoor patio—

Gabe wings a knee over Eric's chest,
Eric grasps for Gabe's face. When finally

I put my hands under Gabe's arms,
gently lift him, I'm amazed

by how light he is, all glamour muscles.
He doesn't know how easily

///

I hold him. When the hero
tells the prince

about the queen-mother's heart,
we forget the multitude of her potential

sorrows. At least she cannot lament
raising a coward. No one calls the cops.

That highly polished sky
catches me looking it in the eye.

## OR AT LEAST TO JUSTIFY THAT BEHAVIOR IN TERMS OF THAT VALUE SYSTEM

Not what words {          } meant
                    mean


                              then, but what they might now.


Darkness between stars,


trust in the sureness of my {                    } ignorance?
                                        inheritance?


                                                      Bootstrap fantasias.


My {          } own
              unknown


                              vast lineages of simplification.—


We think about {          } difference.
                        asterisks.


                              I try every excuse.

## INHERITANCE

Told I am "refusing to identify with whiteness,"
I am so interested in "refusing,"

as if playing a trick or insult,
as if there is no collision

of Jewishness and whiteness—

*A residual nostalgia*
*that displaces /*

*a sense of difference?*
Skim privilege—

that from amnesia rescues—

I have looked for a revealing angel
in artists and poets, in rabbis and moguls,
but who would better serve,
despite himself, than Karl Marx?

*What is the worldly religion of the Jew?*
Marx asks, "On
the Jewish Question."
*Huckstering.*
*What is his worldly God?*
*Money.*

Marx of course
*had been baptized Christian*
*by his Jewish parents,*
along with his parents,

but he came from rabbis on both sides.

"What does one owe one's ignorance?
How does one own one's ignorance?"

Did he have even the self-hate
of alienation?
Or was it plain, his suspicion
of religion as *professional and social convenience,*
or a *necessity to practice the law,*
as it was for his father?


                             *An idealism* that does not
                            *threaten its own style of life . . .*


          could it ever be not merely               —open my heart
                     nostalgic?                     like a vault—


                                   When I say, "Everyone's faith
                                       is personal,"
                             O says, "It's like how I have
                                the one knife I use."

## PHILIP GUSTON

His cartoon Klansmen—smoking
cigars, driving clown cars
littered with liquor bottles—were not
immediately admired.

Playful early lyricism, colorful
and sweet, turned
to ugly pictures, ugly themes.
And what did that make him?
"*A MANDARIN PRETENDING
TO BE A STUMBLEBUM.*"
Did Guston feel guilty,
in later life, for having changed

his name in 1937?
Philip Goldstein would recognize
a mask. I am confused now
over whether it was his past

or abstract expressionism
that inspired Guston

*Related images* / search 'Philip
Guston painting,' / search 'Self-
portrait as Klansman,' / search
'Jews in disguise,'

apologies from athletes, caricatures,
exhortations to find in religious
wisdom codes to generate capital, rich
Jews, rappers and

                      only
one sentimental old painting of a
Jewish moneylender from so long ago
it seems simply a work of shadowy
texture, sociological
                purview—

A kind of false simplicity.

to say, "I got sick
and tired of all that purity!"

*The artist in his studio*
shows a robed Klansman
painting a self-portrait
in Guston's closet.

Guston wondered,
"*What would it be like
to be evil?
To plan, to plot.*"

The same hunched shoulders to mean a Dutch Jew
four hundred years ago, a French Jew two hundred
years later, the same appraising eyes, if not alone
across hundreds of years conspiring together
or lounging before aristocrats,        sources
                of light
           unknown—

                    illumination
into the narrowness      of a window
into the past.

What hasn't just been
auto-filled?

## UNMASKINGS

I knew enough about 'the red scare' to forget it: just another in a long line of reactionary indulgences. A bargain, at twice the price, compared to the pogroms. Harmless enough, clumsy and repudiated.                                    It was called naming names.

"My grandma Fanny used to embarrass my mom," my mother tells me. "She would take her to all these socialist things"—she wasn't a radical, your mom?—"no, no, my mom, she was a liberal. But she was not a radical. Definitely a liberal. She was just, you know . . ."

Is there no way to talk about whiteness without the rhetoric of whiteness?

Functionally
Provisionally
Conditionally
Conveniently

Before the war, I later learned, American Nazis were hired as investigators, called as friendly witnesses in closed rooms by Congressmen wrapped in sham petitions, hunting reds suspicious for being Jews.

At one hearing, an outrageous scheme was 'discovered' in which rich Jews would both manipulate the stock market and hire Spanish mercenaries to overthrow the government.
At another hearing a HUAC member, referring to protesters, swore he had never seen
*such a wilderness of noses in my life.*

"Not 'in-your-face' Judaism, but
she had a strong Jewish identity,"
my mother says, of her mother.

In 1946 one investigator told a professor,
*"You should tell your Jewish friends
that the Jews in Germany
stuck their necks out too far
and Hitler took care of them
and that the same thing will happen here
unless they watch their steps."*

*From the late 1940s to the mid-1950s,*
*over half of Americans associated Jews with*
*communist espionage.*

Water absorbs heat
long before it boils.

*Prominent Jews complained*
*about "the next Commie witness who starts*
*hiding behind his Jewishness . . ."*

## JUST LIKE EVERYONE ELSE, ONLY MORE SO!

*America Is Different*, at first,
the rabbi thinks, but changes
his book's name in reprint:
*The Search for Jewish Identity in
America*. He'd explained the Klan as *in
mid-nineteenth century America,
nativist, antiforeign movements
sprang up, but they were directed
by the Protestant majority, as much
against the Catholics
as against the Jews.*

McCarthy's top prosecutor, Roy Cohn, a Jew; the judge
who sentenced the Rosenbergs, a Jew; of Levittown,
the most famous cookie-cutter suburbs, *William Levitt noted
"No one realizes better than Levitt that an undesirable class
can quickly ruin a community."* Levitt, a Jew, meaning Jews
among others.                Jewish goons hired
by Jewish business-owners    to attack Jewish strikers . . .

On the one hand, very conspicuous ghosts.          Dramatic irony is not moral irony,
On the other, *conceptual nose jobs*.                                but agony
                                                          (*agency is/not
                                            resistance*):

                The red scare led by Congress, but the blacklist
by Jewish Hollywood moguls who feared their power was an illusion:
the start of the movie,
        and not the end:

Jewish communists,              Jewish communists,
during the Depression,          during the Depression,
were often accused of           often changed their names,

changing their names            believing a new name could make
'to hide their true selves      you a better recruiter
doing Satan's work.'            for a better world.

*The trees at the cemetery*
*need trimming*
*and now is the time to do it.*

## THERE ISN'T A LESSON WITHOUT A PRICE?

One space race rabbi
wrote we had
*a built-in*
*middle-class potential—*

Jews classified by early race
'theorists' as Mongolian;

later, *half-Mongol Jews*

. . . *the Jewish race presents the most notorious*
*and least deceptive [example],*

*which can easily be recognized everywhere*
*by their eyes alone,*
*which breathe of the East.*

*. . . cast off the Oriental cloak*

*. . . He still prays in the language of the East,*

*. . . neither of which are any longer used by him.*

*. . . He prays for a speedy return*
*to the Orient, without really meaning a word of it.*

*He prays for an abundance of rain*
*at a time when . . .*

*Emancipation* is the word progressive rabbis used,
having abandoned the traditions
they'd inherited, sacrificing them
for being *outmoded, outlandish—*

~~What it means to be 'good enough, better /~~

~~/ than they thought'?~~

Sacrifices . . . is that what those were?

## 'JEWISH MOTHERS' AND 'TIGER MOMS'

Perhaps it is because we shared a fence with the Wongs / and my sister shared kindergarten through the School of Visual Arts with Jason Wong / and I shared with Lauren Wong kindergarten through the CAPS magnet at our suburban high school across the street from Woodmoor, a neighborhood deed-restricted until just before I was born / perhaps all those years growing up together made my sister enthusiastically insist Asians were

"white like us."

To be white is to see race
as damage.

In 1924 some (few)
Jewish union
leaders supported
a National Origins Act
that would sharply
reduce Jewish
and Asian immigration.
Some (few) had
supported
the Chinese Exclusion
Act in 1882.
Some (few) immigrants
from India
argued in court
that they were Aryan
by name
and descent.

To aspire without realizing it.
~~To not look back.~~

Harvard's *Asian problem*
was once its *Jewish
problem*. Touched by
sympathetic magic,
my sister used to say
our neighbors
"weren't different,
they were Asian."

## COWBOYS AND—

My father married a nice Jewish girl from New Jersey a decade before I was born. When I was 31 he told me, "Do not put this in your poems, cannot prove it, not prejudiced per se, but genteelly racist" speaking softly about his mother and father, Episcopalians from the heartland. His lips barely parted.

Still softly, keeping his eyes on the winding Colorado mountain roads: "They Jewed me down," his mother said, about her friends who owned a corner store in Tulsa. And his father's father: in the Klan in Denver in the '20s? Colorado "a hotbed for it," he whispered.

We are driving from Denver to a cousin's wedding in Estes Park. Trail Ridge Road rising us past forests and tundra.

In Hollywood, Jews *yearning to belong*
were by then beginning to create
the America I thought I knew.

*. . . fashioning a vast, compelling national*
*fantasy out of his dreams*
*and dogmatic faith—*

*a belief in virtue, loyalty, tradition,*
*in America itself.*

*. . . as the outsider's need to hyperbolize*
*and glorify the prevailing culture*
*and its values* mutated

*an America*
*where fathers were strong,*
*families stable, people attractive,*
*resilient, resourceful,*

*and decent.*

I'd been reading aloud: "*For their first march in Houston, in 1921, the Klan wore robes and hoods bought from a Jewish manufacturer.*"

My mother asks
about the Jewish businessmen
who later joined Klan leaders
on bandstands
holding their noses
('hooks' the Klan
would insist),
what choice they had?

My father says: "I consider myself very lucky to have grown up in a family that might have had prejudices, but didn't share them with me."

*Native-born, white, Anglo-Saxon,*
*Protestant Americans* who saw
themselves on screen *could share this*
*fantasy with Mayer and even call it*

*their own.*
*But it is unlikely*
*that any of them could have*
*or would have invented it.*

*To do so, one would have needed the same*
*desperate longing for security*
*that Mayer and so many of the other*
*Hollywood Jews felt . . .*

*One would have had to be so fearful*
*of being outside and alone*
*that one would go to any lengths*
*to fabricate America as a sanctuary . . .*

My father hopes "the kids with Spanish and Indian surnames" in Bartlesville, Oklahoma, where he grew up, "the children of engineers at Phillips experienced neither racism nor class problems."

My mother reminds me that if she'd married
a Jewish man, I would not exist.

I admire most the sweetness
of their naivete, *to present Jews*
*as more American*
*than were native-born whites,*

*precisely because Jewish concerns*
*with social justice heightened their dedication*
*to American ideals*
*of social justice and democracy.*

*"Jews are for killing,"* one Jewish
studio executive of the thirties
*was reported to have said,*
*"not for making movies about."*

G-d, let me use the word
enemies. G-d,
do prayers
have side-effects?

My grandmother—of
blessed memory—her children,
their children:
sweet, good people,
at the wedding shining
love and affection.

In Poland the Jews,
the Cherokee in Oklahoma.
My father raised his children
to be less prejudiced than him.


Many of his friends "claimed a little Indian blood. The Chief of the Cherokee Tribe lived a block over
from your grandmother." He and his brothers shooting imaginary bows and arrows at each other, just
like in the movies, fancying themselves both cowboys and Cherokee?

Could I romanticize
my father,
the un-disappearing
white man?

## BACK(S)LASH

When my father asked me,
"More books full of self-loathing?"
or when a settler colonialist empire
grew addicted to race
as *a way of constructing and mobilizing*
*economic and political rule*
*by referring to " different types of human bodies,"*
racism *central to the regimes of capital*
*accumulation since the country's founding.*

> Do you think G-d reads the holy
> books over and over or
> just once?
>
> G-d can't revise?

Christians / heathens
whites / blacks,
natives / migrants,
whites / white ethnics,
inclusion only ever affirmed
exclusion, the melting pot
erases its erasures—

> Do you think G-d
> glances over a shoulder?
> G-d's shoulder?
>
> Your shoulder?

"pass" long enough
for white,
you're passed, as in
past an
asymmetrical mirror,
but so quick:

"Are you white?" I ask my mom.

"Yes and no . . . it's different
for everyone, and [you]
never know exactly how."

when we see ourselves in it—
the mirror appears clear.

She is right, isn't she, to say
she's "blessed" she "didn't
experience discrimination"?

Awake to a spell of bubble wrap.

Amnesias of assimilation?
*Even in nineteenth century Germany*
*Jewish migrants were singing*
*"a man is worth what he is, and he is*
*what he does. Before all else, be free—*
*and go to America."*

What do I repress? What do I
deny? As if G-d won't hear
what I keep silent.

Who do I betray, as if when I
speak . . .

*. . . and whose work explicitly opposes*
*the notion of a hierarchy of oppressions,*
*even as I find them*
*within myself.*
*Thirty-three, I wear*
*my Rockets hat*

as a yarmulke, swear my curls
start to come back.
As if reduced to the part of me
that dreams of looking down
on my father?
What wickedness would I be
to imagine one part of me
less than another?

And then my father mentions
a book I have never heard of.
"A remembrance. By my great-
great-great-grandfather David.
From the Shuey side
of the family. My father's
mother," he explains.
"Their journey started in 1865,
he and his brother, Natural
Bridge, Virginia,"
and I shiver.
"No reference to the war
or what they did
during the war. The town
in a hilly, rocky area, wooded,
not agricultural, not
plantation land," my father
clarifies.
There is, it turns out,

"Do you realize that tiger lilies
from your Bar Mitzvah
are still blooming in our yard?"
He tells me
about lilacs, tulips, daffodils.
"The tiger lilies aren't
particularly sweet.
My garden doesn't smell this
much this time of year.
My compost pile
has an odor."
Finally, he says again,
he'll look for the book.
But he doesn't want to talk
about his grandparents.
"I'm more interested
in making today and tomorrow
better. I can't do anything about
the sins
of the past,
but I can try to prevent
sins of the future."

Once I'd asked why he never
told me about Black Wall
Street, the massacre 40 miles
from Bartlesville, Oklahoma.
He asked, "Did it happen
before I was born?

"Now, Boulder was a
sundown town," he says, his
father's father's sun. "I can't
speak for them.
'They had to be patient
to get their rights' . . . Black
people," he explains, that's
something he knew his
grandparents thought, but
"impossible

he remembers,
"reference to 'a trusty
servant,' the term
used by whites then
because they did not
want to say slave."
A possibility I had
chosen not
to imagine, not even
once. "They lived
in West Bridge
Country,
the western half
of the state.
They trekked West,
end up in Colorado,
Oklahoma." Naïve
to the forces carrying
them?

(No.)

"The family history box,
it seems to have just
disappeared.

"Vanished. Clippings
of newspaper stories,
[yellowed? crumbling
through fingers?]
grandmother's writing,
memories,
great-grandfathers.

"It was in the office, I
distinctly remember it
being in the office.

"And that's what we can't
figure out.
What happened?

"We will find it."

without proof."
They can't defend
themselves; self-
censorship as seemingly
ethical stance?

Almost summer.
"I'm not
a green thumb, no
patience.
I just plant
and what comes up
comes up."
Dresses, letters, furs,
poems, everything
lost and un-burned,
strip *the sacred aura
of the absent
ordinary* away. That's
not enough.
The missing,
forgotten, shamed,
loose sheets,
paper-clipped.
It didn't even
have a cover.

## HAVE I ALWAYS BEEN SUSPICIOUS OF MYSELF?

The rainy day my parents married,
my father signed two contracts:
one with my mother,
the other with her rabbi.
Because they loved each other,
the first contract.
Because I was raised Jewish,
the second.
History moves this way, backwards,
precarious. Not passing
but passed.
Almost writing to him about 'your

|  |  |
|---|---|
| | Why did I ever think I |
| | would know myself |
| like Talmud | |
| | when I don't/know Talmud? |

forebears' instead of 'our—'
My dad asking, "When were Swedes
considered white?"
What description isn't
incomplete? I talk like him, I write
like him, I too
have what he calls his father's
coldness. Pathologically
consistent, how unfair am I
to not be him, after all?
To regret he had no lone faith
for me to reject. All his life
he's been a searcher.

| | ~~Though I am~~ |
|---|---|
| ~~made beautiful by righteous~~ | |
| | ~~anger, it means that from a distance~~ |
| ~~I give two names.~~ | |
| | ~~I'm selfish,~~ |
| ~~I am, I always have been.~~ | |
| | ~~Still there's no consensus~~ |
| ~~about my highest point.~~ | |

|  |  |
|---|---|
| | Who can blame me? |
| | Last night I remarked to the snow |
| that it doesn't need | |
| | the sky. |

## THE NATURAL WORLD

It turns out roadrunners are not blue,
or perpetually hounded by coyotes.
My childhood hypothesis

that bees sting the flowers
taunts me still, and echolocation,
Owen tries to teach me,

is not just a simile. "It's so weird
having a kid who still thinks the world
is a great place," Lauren says.

Einstein wrote of *real difficulty*
*in that physics is a kind of metaphysics;*
*physics describes 'reality.' We don't know*

*what 'reality' is; we know it*
*only by means of the physical description.*
Bedtime stories,

euphemisms, as if gravity
can be explained away.
He's heard of Nazis,

watched superheroes
beat them up in cartoons;
thinks jail is a game

where kids lock
their parents up, lie down
and snore until the parents

sneak back to their adult
politics. When he told us
the 'I' went missing

at pre-school,
he meant a laminated shape
he could barely recognize

had been hidden,
and he wants to find it so bad
he'll learn how to spell.

We can't escape the literal,
so we try again, we tell him
some people are judged

by the color of their skin,
his friends, their families.
He's been learning cactus facts,

how hawks perceive earth's
magnetic field, honeybees
flap their wings

two hundred and thirty times
a second. Likely
he'll forget we ever had

this conversation.
He nods, says he has
lots of friends.

He will grow up in Houston
thinking he's living in the future.
For now he absorbs

every kind of dinosaur.
And how to grow a lemon tree.

///////////////////////////

> "One must never forget his fellow man, regardless of race, creed, or color."
>
> —General Maurice Hirsch
>
> hosted a weekly open house in his River Oaks home, sweetheart rose in the lapel of his vested suit. (One of the first to buy, having married a non-Jew.)

> In college Hirsch writes in his journal:
> *"You can't misunderstand a surface."*

On the one hand, his foresight. On the other, our hindsight.

He was a Harvard man, he fought the Nazis, he opened up River Oaks.
If I offer up this man.

And *The Jewish Mothers Hall of Fame.*

My furrier great-grandfather catching a robber
at Yankee Stadium, during the seventh inning stretch.

The orange index card: *Josh's favorite*,
parenthetical, after *arlene's apple pie.*

A brief explanation of the artist's context, what is called didactic text:
Where and when the artist was born. The title of the art. Materials used.                    (Tombstones.)

A sentiment is ironized.
      Making art is doing self-criticism.
            Calling it art allows it to be dismissed.

If I offer up my childhood nicknames:
Spike, Tank, Spiketank, Bearclaw, the Vanilla Knish.

And that there is no commandment
to be funny.

If I am offered up,                                                           What father
as a joke.                                                           has no understudy?

///////////////////////////

## THE GULF

Dybbuk says G-d's a wave,
fast and in a straight line,
downhill. Lectures me
on my disbelief. He's obsessed,

I think. For school
Owen needs to record
traditions. Our family tree, origins.
"Boundaries, boundaries, boundaries,"

Owen sings, when I cling to him
by the seawall. Lauren's rainbow dragon kite
races behind us, in sunlight-
smothered gray-cold clouds.

We lost a kite last New Year's here,
it happens that quick. "Be careful,"
Owen warns, seven times he warns us,
about the kite. I'm the same way.

Owen's never asked who he is,
he's not yet so caught up
in loss. "Waves crash on the seawall,"
Owen says, on his tiptoes at the edge,

"they're consumed by bigger waves,
which crash to be ate again."
We promise to map what we know
about his past, tomorrow. (I'd hoped

my grandfather's brother
could tell us about him.
"We were five years apart," he'd said,
"we weren't that close.")

Tonight we'll drive along the beach,
watch for stars and fireworks,
like we did last year.
Even here, on the Gulf,

constellations cease to be,
single stars linked by
denuded sky.
Guessing up at them now,

through the gray,
why do I think dybbuk
was a sinner
to possess me?

## BIBLES

I felt sorry for her, my grandmother:
*The Bible for Dummies* lay on her coffee table,
surrounded by old issues of *Life* and *Time*.
Dust shimmered on those closed covers,

Oklahoma sun poking through closed blinds.
Her children mostly lived nearby.
We stayed a coast away, and when she died
I was young enough to mistake as well

| How do my dead pray for me? |
| --- |
| And why? |
| To what sacredness praise my ordinary life? |

| Why waste on me<br><br>their prayers? |
| --- |
| Once again the leaves change color cannot be all there is |

our plane through gray clouds
descending blue sky
as metaphor where there was
only loss. On the coffee table still,

*The Bible for Dummies*, buried in dust.
It was blasphemy, once, to believe
the Torah was not dictated literally
at Mount Sinai. The Rabbis say the day

the Torah translated into Greek
was as dark for the Jews
as when the Golden Calf
shined out against the mountainside.

Torah winds inside Tanakh.
The word 'Orthodox' is Greek,
it means correct thoughts.
In English, I mean, it means.

| only apples and oranges<br><br>are like apples and oranges |
| --- |
| I try to understand.<br>I can know Y-u, |

G-d,


by not knowing Y-u?

I praise Y-u
in a tongue not my own?

I could be so pious
I'd summon an angel
to better learn Torah.
But I've never been so pious.

I wish I felt
the angel we summon
is within ourselves,
but it's just an ordinary angel.

## WHAT I AM AN ALLEGORY FOR REMAINS A MYSTERY TO ME

Thousands of words
passed down
from Mount Sinai?
And years
through prophets
and scribes,
editors and copyists,
a single error
—one wrong letter
—seen as sin?
I don't doubt Jonah
would run
from G-d's
transcription.

There's much I {        } doubt.
                          don't doubt.
Since when is lack of purpose
a reward?
Before Ivrim meant Hebrews,
the word was 'transcenders,'
traveling from place to place.
I want to believe
in more than one kind
of portable homeland.
Sitting in the shade
of the ruined plant,
devote myself
to something inside me
that is also above me—

An altar used to mean to
make a site of sacrifice.
What are {        } Y-u
bringing here? What are
       {        } you
letting go?

## REPENTANCE

Today I learned portion
and interpretation have the same root.
Words wander away from each other,
but they're family still, at heart.

Jonah in the belly of the whale.
I wonder at the difference
between the plain
and the deep esoteric reading.

My son tells me he's afraid
of what comes after
life. A split, a severing,
the surface vast.
Sometimes we read books
where people die.
I struggle saying "die."
"Gone," "left," I try

all kinds of {              } mis-direction
                                routes.

Owen likes to read ahead.
What's beneath the surface?
I read to him what he's already read.
He knows what happens next.

Some words appear once only
in the Torah. Unique,
we guess at what they mean.
And what about us

appearing once {        } only?
                            lonely?

Jonah in the belly of the whale, still
Jonah on land, giving the plain reading.

## NO PAINTER WOULD HIDE ME IN A BLUE FLOWER

"If we're not gentle
we can't play burial,"
Lauren said, after I shrieked
from under the pile
of stuffed animals
Owen had jumped into.

of compassion
as the apex of justice;

No, more than pious,
with the fanaticism

My son loves me
violently. Laughing,
he hit me so hard today
he hurt his arm.
Laughing and moaning
he kept swinging.

someday. I hope he is
better than me.

I hope you're less damaged
than me, I'll tell my son

"You're fine!" he yelled,
his mouth open like a shark's.
I let him hit me. He had to stand
on my bed to tackle me.
"It's just pretend," he said,
bringing me to one knee.

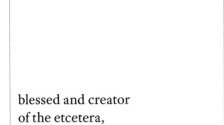

blessed and creator
of the etcetera,

and call it
prayer (etc.)

## AS IF YOU YOURSELF FLED EGYPT FORTY YEARS

At temple Friday I wrestled with the feather
I'm meant to search the Torah
with—there can't be anything extra
in the Torah—so I asked a stranger
why I'm a perfectionist in everything
but belief. All Sabbath, I made excuses—
I had dishes in the sink, essays to grade—
as if it's a matter of finding time
for G-d, as if a stranger
was living my life, wasting my Sabbath.
There can't be anything extra in the world,
yet every generation of Jews lives inside us.
On one hand, what I profess to love;
on the other, every distraction: poker, TV movies,
games of hoops I'm cursed to claim
as aesthetic events.
This morning I take my son
to Sunday school, the children's service,
in the same room where I promised
I'd comb my soul just two nights ago.
Now the cantor asks us to sing along,
I sing along to a song for children,
and the youth leaders do a silly dance,
I dance along, next to my son.
During call and response,
I call and I respond.
The rabbi teaches the children a story
I heard when I was a child,
about an old man who has no room in his heart
for anyone but himself, who is forced
to live like a beggar for a week,
while an angel sleeps in his fancy house.
The moral is obvious
even to me with my forty years
of facts, history, and commentary;
I might as well be a child again.
We each take what we can
from the angels that visit us.
We are as worthy Sunday morning
as we were Friday night,

when we believed we could change,
we could be better, praise
spilling from our lips,
we could worship hard enough
to make us worthy.

## STILL THE ARROW OF THE SUN WHILES AWAY ON THE LAKE I WOKE UP TO BE PIERCED BY

Armed with seven names
for G-d I felt like a fraud
correcting the spelling in my note

at the Western Wall. Praying
my few Hebrew phrases
(supplied by Lubavitchers).

Your mother danced
(in the women's section),
I felt like a hole in the wall.

But a few days earlier, when we'd landed,
when the bus crested the bell
of the hill, the bell

of my blood rang. Then
I thought I'd wake in time
to join your mother

for that first sunrise.
I dreamed of faces
upturned in Jerusalem,

our gun-toting medic
joked about his face, twisted
to a blizzard

after a week of rain
precipitating our arrival,
night already settled,

and then the rain,
oh yes, the Galilee Sea, oh,
the Kinnerit, stray birds turning

inward, centered, mocking the water
reflecting the light
all night lying awake

on the stuttering Galilee.
I thought you'd be born
in Jerusalem.

I don't blame you for that.
This morning you marched
the perimeter of our courtyard patio,

an unseasonably pleasant day
in April, in Houston,
where your mother has a good job

and I have a good job and we both
speak the language, blowing
on your purple plastic shofar

and muttering to yourself,
"Let my people go."
We had driven roads there

of destroyed cities,
along vineyard land fallow
for hundreds of years, or so

I'd been told.
Don't ask me the wishes
I crumpled and stuffed

into stone. And then
we were no longer
at the ancient temple.

What we miss
is always that
quick. Unroll me,

      give me your blessing.

## WE SHOULD FEEL BETTER ABOUT SELF-KNOWLEDGE

Through the blinds this morning, sun
pressed up against the window, liquid
gold, then as the sun rose
the bottom of the window was only
filled with light, where the top
was bursting still. Skyscrapers,
G-d prefers mountains
humble. The morning
undone little by little.

Once, at the Grand Canyon,
we trekked from our cabin
to the rim of night,
watched a garbage truck
pull up to the dumpster behind
El Tovar Dining Room,
its claws shaking trash in
as day crawled up overhead.
I wondered if the driver was awed
every day, or had long since learned
to look away. Reading

what G-d does and doesn't want
again, while the quality of the light
changes, while the blinds build a fence
around the window.

My son is old enough to teach me
how to make a paper airplane,
paper jet, add a paperclip
to the nose for weight.
I'd forgot how, I admit it.
The rabbis prayed,
while over their heads
an aircraft disappeared
from one window to another
and another, as they sang;
gray plane flush with tall clouds
reappearing until it summitted
our view. A marvel:

Once, at the Grand Canyon,
he got close to the edge
—now that memory
disappears as he gets older,
though we remind him.
We thought
he'd never forget
the Grand Canyon,
for years he'd tell us
how he took in
the vast
emptiness before him,
unafraid, and small.

*"The ways we have wronged Y-u,
through insincere apologies."*

Call and response—
we are meant
to repent—I lost
my place, and repeated
myself; they'd all
moved on.

That's when I felt closest to Y-u,
when Y-u caught me.

On vellum and paper,
papyrus and cloth,
over a thousand years
of words
fragmented by time,
studied for over
a hundred years,
even still
we recover whole
poems, letters, prayers,
each time
'a new join'
is found.

this architecture, this temple:
hierarchies of sun
through high-set

windows, geometries
of floor and ceiling conspire
light into a flood

descending down an altar
elevated to the ark,
its crown. Outside, too,

the plane flew.

## RACHEL COULD HAVE LANDED HERE (GALVESTON BEACH, TEXAS)

I'm puzzled, most of all,
by my own {          } instance,
                          insistence—

As if my son won't only ever
be himself. Looking at the Gulf he asks me,
"What's the point of a mountain
you can't climb?"

> If not 100 blessings a day, say
>
> 10 blessings, 1 blessing.

Add a {          } ladder
              letter
                      to a word in your mind.

I want to be rebuked by a G-d
who struggles with me.
"Keep shoveling," Owen insists,
sand giving way to more sand.

Lauren has been teaching Owen to not kill
plants, ants, bluebonnets. "Landscape
is the friend to clarity," my rabbi {          } prays
                                                          craves.

They can't all be opinions—
the winds and the waves,
sun under stone.

> If not 100 blessings a day, say
>
> 10 blessings, 1 blessing.

This is a weird place
to put things in perspective because
you can't get any distance from them.

A pelican soars by, its stilled wings outstretched.

We sit and look at the water.

## GLOSS

I knew it must have been important
that my mother would let my son
cross the street alone

in my dream. We'd rented a house
big enough for Thanksgiving,
close to the beach, and I couldn't tell

cars from waves, lying there in the dark.
Three bright busy lanes,
the cars screaming by, why was she

letting him go like that?
I wanted to scream at her
in the dream.

Was I asleep? I was alone.

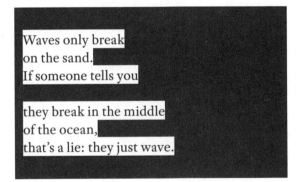

Waves only break
on the sand.
If someone tells you

they break in the middle
of the ocean,
that's a lie: they just wave.

She shouldn't have been here,
my mother, sick with who knows what.
A kind but busy woman;

they'd gone straight to the airport
from the doctor.
She yelped when I touched her head

where the doctor had worked.

In the morning I snuck past the room
where my son dragged his mother,
sleepwalking. Avoided mirrors,

ran to the beach; pounded
my feet into the sand.
No child wants to bury a parent.

When the temple filled with sacrifices,
what prayers kept them then?

I imagine silence.

A glowing darkness.
A wave breaking
in the middle of the ocean.

## THE HARVEST FESTIVAL

As a rule, I don't write poems
about the moon. Over
the grocery store
that used to be a movie theater,
the marquee shines its white lights.
My son always says,
"But there's one thing,"
in the middle of an argument.
It's never just one thing.
He'll say it again and again,
if we're not listening.
Prayer, too, repeats itself.
I guess we've been walking a while now,
finding a view.
I'm trying to listen, I swear.


Lately I've been lined,
exposed. Waiting
for test results,
job offers.
Walking, I used to worry
about my son's
sudden movements.
Now he watches me
for inconsistencies.


The dark repeats around us.
I wonder why I ever thought
more is hidden than revealed.
I could call those lights neon,
but who knows? There's a name for that,
something old that's no longer what it was,
but just like it was, autumn
on its way, almost analogous.

Translation fails when the word
could only ever mean itself:
"l'chaim" turned to "cheers"
instead of, "to life."
Moses read the Torah
from behind a veil
for fear
of being blinded.


There's always been a world
behind the world.
Jacob, wrestling the angel,
didn't see a ladder,
but a ziggurat.
Whenever someone spies
the reality behind reality
it's with their own eyes.

**SHIBBOLETHS**

"It's like I was a coin and the world
was a magnet," Owen says,
after riding a bike for the first time.

Sun's down to that magic height
where the live oaks catch its blaze;
we just get its shine. He's racing

again, yelling at me
not to chase him.
He has my thick skull,

laugh, eyelashes; my dad
called me Tank,
I call him Pinball—

the world is a magnet I think
about grinding my teeth
when he was a baby, still

he careens, whistling
along, speeds like air
through G-d's lips.

*Wonder rather than doubt*
*is the root of all knowledge*

We shout for him to stop;
will he carry my hunger
to please? My worship

of teachers? Will he over-think,
like me, or will he agonize?
He's got my legs,

his eyes, I know it's wrong                    but doubt
to look for belief
in a lock of hair,                                    is the root of all wonder.

any natural ease of faith
I lack. Will my skepticism
be his patrimony? Who am I

to tell him who we are?
"We are overtime!" Owen yells,
rides infinite imperfect circles,

around us, un-alone.

## WHEN A CLOUD IS NOT AN ORANGE

In the book I had just read to Owen,
he marveled at a tree animals used

as a library,
and now he is climbing a tree,

picking oranges
in the courtyard of the temple,

where every year he learns his name
has been inscribed in the book of life.

I have been so disconnected
from the natural world

I had never thought about oranges
starting green.

Most fruits start green,
but not clouds. My son's mind

takes on the many aspects
of the cloud; he is telling me

the clouds look like clouds,
when I ask him what they look like.

Then he tells me, "respect
means practicing good manners

so G-d doesn't stay away,"
and I wonder if I missed something,

looking at the clouds, thinking
oranges should taste orange,

shouldn't they? Owen climbs
higher to pick another green orange,

he has yet to be convinced

his senses can disagree

with what he knows is true. I don't care
if a book is a kind of simulation,

more porous than I ever
would have guessed.

"Orange!" Owen says,
over and over,

willing the green to shift
before his eyes.

## ACKNOWLEDGMENTS

I am grateful to the editors of the following journals, where some of these poems appeared: *ANMLY*: "Conversion," "New prayer book," and "Belief to me a kind of Sabbath work." *Barzakh*: "Microwave." *Berru Poetry Series*: "Silent partner." *Concision*: "Have I always been suspicious of myself?" and "Rachel could have landed here." *Dream Pop*: "Continuity theory" and "Philip Guston." *Ekphrasis Magazine*: "Rothko before the color fields" (previously titled "Authenticity"). *ferry me magazine*: "We should feel better about self-knowledge." *Hayden's Ferry Review*: "Metropolis Golem." *Image*: "Still the arrow of the sun whiles away on the lake I woke up to be pierced by." *Ilanot Review*: "When a cloud is not an orange." *"Jewish Currents*: "Chain migration." *Jewish Literary Journal*: "Shibboleths." *Marrow*: "Meet the teachers night." *Otiyot*: "The harvest festival," "Great mystics," "Gloss," and "The Sabbath approaches." *Poet Lore*: "No painter would hide me in a blue flower." *Superstition Review*: "A geniza" and "Jewish exorcism."

I am also grateful to the editors of the following anthologies for including poems from this book: The Laurel Review's *Breaking the Glass: A Contemporary Jewish Poetry Anthology*: "Repentance," "What I am an allegory for remains a mystery to me," and "When flight was a miracle, navigators dignified the stars by hand." *Odes and Elegies: Eco-Poetry from the Texas Gulf Coast*: "It privileges land to say ghost trees."

I am especially grateful to Suzanna Tamminen for believing in *Dybbuk Americana* and for wise editorial guidance, as well to as the staff of Wesleyan University Press for making the book possible. The work that went into this publication is greatly appreciated. Thank you also to Jim Schley for meeting this challenging manuscript with attention and care.

This book could not have been written without the generous support of the University of Houston Creative Writing Program, Inprint, and the Yiddish Book Center.

Many teachers have been instrumental in my journey as a poet, especially my dissertation committee: Kevin Prufer, Hayan Charara, Sarah Ehlers, and Maeera Shreiber. Gratitude also to Martha Serpas, Tony Hoagland, Nick Flynn, Roberto Tejada, Erin Belieu, Josh Lambert, Lisa Olstein, and my first teachers: Lucille Clifton, Edgar Silex, and Jeffrey Coleman. Thank you to Carl Lindahl for teaching me folklore.

Special thanks to my meticulous, thoughtful readers, especially Allison Pitinii Davis, Niki Herd, Stalina Villarreal, Lau Cesarco Eglin, Glenn Shaheen, Brandon Lamson, and Lauren Berry. Discussions with scholars, writers, and other interlocutors also proved inspiring; thank you to Charlotte Wyatt, Jessamine Batario, Liza Watkins, Nick Rattner, Cait Weiss, Brandon White, Sehban Zaidi, Toni Fields Wilson, and David Segal. Thank you to Carrie Ermler—the back desk of the Menil Collection saw many revisions of this book.

Librarians, archivists, and curators suggested books, dug into microfilm with me, and offered invaluable advice. Thank you to Catherine Essinger, Emily Deal, Judy Weidman, Jon Evans, Marie Wise, and Josh Furman.

Thank you to Marilyn Hassid, Janice Rubin, Rich Levy, Isabelle Ganz, Gail Klein, Bruce Stein, and the rabbis Kenny and Amy Weiss, whose insight into Houston's Jewish community helped shape my thinking for this book, as well as the welcoming rabbinical team at Temple Emanu El.

Thank you to my parents, Arlene Gottlieb and Chaz Miller.

Lauren, you make me a better person and poet.

Owen, this book is for you.

# READINGS

Poetry in this book builds on scholarship ranging from art history to anthropology, Jewish studies to literary criticism, as well as a variety of religious texts. The following are the sources I studied most closely while writing *Dybbuk Americana*:

Baigell, Matthew. *Jewish Artists in New York during the Holocaust Years*. Washington, DC: Center for Advanced Holocaust Studies, 2001.

Bloom, Solomon F. "Karl Marx and the Jews." *Jewish Social Studies* 4, no. 1 (January 1942): 3–16. (See "Inheritance.")

Brodkin, Karen. *How Jews Became White Folks and What That Says About Race in America*. New Brunswick: Rutgers University Press, 1998. (See "A double bind" and "Is it wrong that I find comfort in finding myself.")

Cohen, Anne Nathan. *The Centenary History: Congregation Beth Israel of Houston, Texas 1854–1954*. Houston: Congregation Beth Israel, 1954.

Cole, Peter, and Adina Hoffman. *Sacred Trash: The Lost and Found World of the Cairo Geniza*. New York: Nextbook/Schocken, 2011.

Dennis, Rabbi Geoffrey W. *The Encyclopedia of Jewish Myth, Magic and Mysticism*. Woodbury, MN: Llewellyn Publications, 2007. (See "(Purim is taught)" and "How to read the dybbuk.")

Feiffer, Jules. Interview by Christa Whitney on November 1, 2017, in *Jules Feiffer's Oral History*. Wexner Oral History Project, The Yiddish Book Center. www.yiddishbookcenter.org/collections/oral-histories/interviews/woh-fi -0000994/jules-feiffer-2017. Accessed 19 March 2021.

Fielder, Brigitte. *Relative Races, Genealogies of Interracial Kinship in Nineteenth-Century America*. Durham: Duke University Press, 2020.

Fredman, Stephen. *A Menorah for Athena: Charles Reznikoff and the Jewish Dilemmas of Objectivist Poetry*. Chicago: University of Chicago Press, 2001.

Gabler, Neal. *An Empire of Their Own: How the Jews Invented Hollywood*. New York: Anchor, 1989. (See "Unmaskings," "Just like everyone else, only more so!," and "Cowboys and—.")

Goldin, Judah, translator. Illustrated by Ben-Zion. *The Living Talmud: The Wisdom of the Fathers and Its Classical Commentaries*. New York: The Heritage Press, 1960. (See "Spirit, breath, or wind.")

Harel, Omri, and Gil Kidron. "25: Jacob and the Supernatural." *A Podcast of Biblical Proportions*. September 8, 2021. Podcast, MP3 audio, 31:25. https:// podcastofbiblicalproportions.com/patriarchs%3A-jacob/. (See "The harvest festival.")

Hirsch, Maurice. Unpublished journals. The Museum of Fine Arts Houston Archives.

Horowitz, Sara R. "The Paradox of Jewish Studies in the New Academy." In *Insider/Outsider: American Jews and Multiculturalism*, edited by David Biale, Michael Galchinsky, and Susannah Heschel, 116–30. Berkeley: University of California Press, 1998.

Hurst, Alexander. "'I felt like an impostor': a mixed-race American in Africa." London: *The Guardian*. December 2018. (See "White ethnics.")

Libenson, Dan, and Lex Rofeberg. "314: Leonard Cohen, and Other Rabbis: Harry Freedman." *Judaism Unbound*. February 18, 2022. Podcast, MP3 audio, 51:54. www.judaismunbound.com/podcast/episode-314-harry-freedman/. (See "Bibles.")

Ostriker, Alicia. "'Howl' Revisited: The Poet as Jew," *The American Poetry Review* 26, no. 4 (July/August 1997): 28–31. (See "(In narrative start as late as possible/In history as early).")

Nelson, Cary. "Lyric Politics: The Poetry of Edwin Rolfe," Introduction to *Trees Became Torches: Selected Poems*. Edited by Cary Nelson, Edwin Rolfe, and Jefferson Hendricks, 1–39. Urbana: University of Illinois Press, 1995. (See "Just like everyone else, only more so!")

Painter, Nell Irvin. *The History of White People*. New York: W. W. Norton & Company, 2011. (See "Back(s)lash.")

Rosenberg, Stuart E. *America Is Different: The Search for Jewish Identity in America*. London: Thomas Nelson & Sons, 1964. (See "Just like everyone else, only more so!" and "There isn't a lesson without a price?")

Schjeldahl, Peter. "The Junkman's Son," *New Yorker*, November 3, 2003. (See "Philip Guston.")

Schwarz, Karl. *Jewish Artists of the 19th and 20th Centuries*. New York: Philosophical Library, 1949.

Stevens, Garry. *The History in the Bible*. Podcast, MP3 audio, various episodes. www.historyinthebible.com/. (See "What I am an allegory for remains a mystery to me.")

Stone, Bryan Edward. *The Chosen Folks: Jews on the Frontiers of Texas*. Austin: University of Texas Press, 2013. (See "Conquistadors," "Rejected Jewish girls," "I wonder at his Hebrew name but do not ask," and "Cowboys and—.")

Trachtenberg, Joshua. *Jewish Magic and Superstition: A Study in Folk Religion*. PhD diss, Columbia University; New York: Behrman's Jewish Book House, 1939; reprint London: Forgotten Books, 2007.

Zangwill, Israel. *The Melting-Pot*. Project Gutenberg. Release Date: December 18, 2007. EBook #23893, www.gutenberg.org/files/23893/23893-h/23893-h.htm/.

**ARCHIVES**

Library and Archive, Congregation Beth Israel Hyman Judah Schachtel, Houston, Texas.

Archives, Museum of Fine Arts, Houston.

South Texas Jewish History Archive, Rice University.

Special Collections, University of Houston Libraries.

**FAMILY PAPERS, ORAL HISTORIES**

Gottlieb, Arlene. Interview by Joshua Gottlieb-Miller, February 26, 2017. Interview, transcript, and recording in author's collection.

Gottlieb, Sidney. Interview by Joshua Gottlieb-Miller, January 22, 2019. Interview, transcript, and recording in author's collection.

Sobel, Edith. Interviews by Joshua Gottlieb-Miller, January 14, 2019. Interviews 1 and 2, transcripts, and recordings in author's collection.

Sobel, Edith. Letters and eulogy from a personal collection.

## ABOUT THE AUTHOR

JOSHUA GOTTLIEB-MILLER is the author of *The Art of Bagging* (2023), which won Conduit's Marystina Santiestevan First Book Prize. His poetry, essays, scholarship, hybrid, and multimedia writing has also been published in *Brooklyn Rail*, *Image*, *Poet Lore*, *Pleiades*, and *Breaking the Glass: A Contemporary Jewish Poetry Anthology*, among other venues, and previously he served as Digital Nonfiction Editor and Poetry Editor at *Gulf Coast*. He has been awarded support from the University of Houston, Yiddish Book Center, MacDowell Colony, Yetzirah, and elsewhere. From 2018–2019 he was an inaugural Post-Harvey Think Tank Fellow at Rice University's Humanities Research Center, representing folklore. He serves on the faculty at San Jacinto College.